IF I DIE YOUNG

Words and Music by
KIMBERLY PERRY

Slowly ♩ = 69

Chorus:

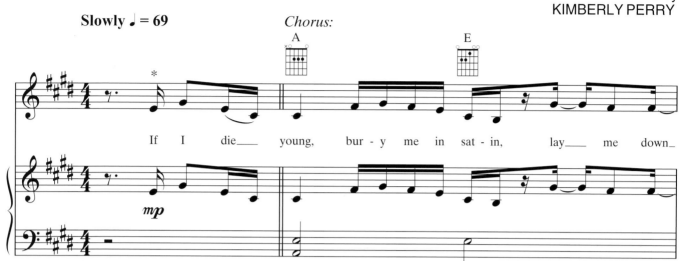

If I die___ young, bur-y me in sat-in, lay___ me down___

___ on a bed of ros-es, sink___ me in the riv-er at dawn,___ send___ me a-

way___ with the words of a love song. Uh oh,_____ uh oh.____

*All vocals written at pitch.

If I Die Young - 8 - 1

Verse 1:

Verse 2:

Well, I've____ had__ just e - nough time.__

So put on your best__ boys and I'll wear my pearls.

8